A Plan Undone

Christopher Holdstrom

BLUEPRINT PRESS
INTERNATIONALE

A Plan Undone
Copyright © 2023 by Christopher Holdstrom

ISBN
978-1-961117-07-5 (Paperback)
978-1-961117-08-2 (eBook)
978-1-961117-06-8 (Hardcover)

To those who i love more
Melissa & Suzanna
who showed me hope
Mom & Dad
who taught me never to give up

Table of Contents

JEREMIAH

*For I know the plans that I have for you –
declares the Lord – plans to prosper you, not to
harm you, plans to give you hope and a future...*

Chapter twenty-nine, verse 11 (NIV)

Prologue

I lie face down. The floor is cold. Morning sunlight spills through the open window blinds. Streams of light and shadow cast about the room. I don't know who I am, where I am, or what I am. Ideas splinter unrestrained about my brain. My mind cannot keep pace. Transient thoughts revolve quickly and randomly in bizarre and delusional ways—they repeatedly surface, peak and dissipate. I'm all-powerful one moment—wiser than any mortal. The next moment I'm weak and alone—a damned fool buried in a torrent of thoughts. Weak, weaker, failing, failed. Nothing can break the torment. I'm a saint one moment—the world adores me. The next moment I lay frail and dying—the world would have me dead.

A small wooden pencil lies at the foot of the bed beside me. I pick up the pencil and write. There is no paper. I write on the walls. I write about Trigonometry and Geometry and Calculus—on proofs, theorems, and equations. I write about Philosophy and Ethics—Can a good man with good intentions go off the path of righteousness and still be considered good? I write for hours. My mind skips randomly from topic to topic but through it all I find a trace of sanity. Behind a glass window—a small, bearded man sits reading. He looks up from his clipboard, pushes his black, horn-rimmed glasses to the bridge of his nose and nods. I hear the door behind me unlock and open.

"Hello Christopher, my name is Dr. Stabler. I'm here to help you. Do you know where you are? You're at Addison Gilbert Hospital in Gloucester, Massachusetts—the psychiatric ward, Walker II. You're in the right place. You've been through quite an ordeal. Here, take these. They'll help you sleep. You need to rest."

Two M&M's in a paper thimble, water in a paper cup. I pop the pills in my mouth, and drink from the cup. The taste is brackish and stale—like seawater. I hear the door close behind me. Once again, I am locked within.

My thoughts spiral and race. One moment I'm a prophet—the world awaits my epistle. The next moment I'm a criminal—the world would have me crucified. Oh Lord, where are you? What have I done? Why have You abandoned me? I'm sick and delirious—beyond exhaustion. At last, the meds kick in. They suppress my craze. The irrational, unrelenting thoughts abate. The meds overwhelm me beyond my illness—they shut me down completely. I slump clumsily to the floor. I lay unconscious until dawn the next day.

| # Without a Burden

God is great. God is good. I have more stars on the Sunday school attendance chart than almost any kid my age. I go to Sunday school most every week. At Sunday school I learn to love God. I learn that God loves me. God created me for a reason. Somehow, He will use me. I'll never know His plan in this life, but I'll follow His plan so long as I pray to Him for direction. I never think much about the Lord's plan for me but I believe and I trust God. I pray to God every night as I lie in bed. I have confidence that God will watch over me and protect me.

Life is good. I have two older brothers and two loving parents. Mom is my caretaker. She takes me with her almost everywhere she goes—shopping, visiting friends, relaxing at the town beach in summer. When I get into mischief, she laughs at me. When I'm sick or tired, she's comforts me. She's fun and outgoing—active in our Church and local community. She seems to know almost everyone in town.

Dad's an engineer. He always has one or more projects going on in or around our home. He can fix almost anything, sometimes with—and other times despite—my older brothers' help. Away from work and home, Dad spends time serving the Lord as moderator at the local Church we attend. Dad is polite and courteous in public, a pillar of the Church. He's a big man—six feet tall and close to 250 pounds. His size is intimidating—he dwarfs me and my brothers. When he speaks, I listen. When he tells me to do something I do it. When he's angry, Dad's voice bellows as loud as a grizzly bear. He doesn't yell at me much. But he yells a lot —most often at my brothers.

"You boys are older. You should know better than this. Act your age. Set an example for your younger brother."

My brothers don't seem to mind the hollering much—they do as they please. My oldest brother, Dave, is a budding entomologist. He carries a butterfly net with him most everywhere he goes. My other brother, Dan, builds model rockets, cars and airplanes—a next generation engineer. As brothers we rarely fight. But when Dad demands an answer as to who's thrown a baseball through the front window of our house—or who's responsible for leaving his tools outside in the rain—the finger pointing begins. Dan accuses Dave. Dave blames Dan. I just shrug my shoulders and stay out of the fray.

As I get older, I have certain talents. I'm among the brighter kids in my class at Steward Elementary School in Topsfield, Massachusetts. I play games and sports with my two older brothers and their friends—to be older, smarter, and stronger. We play street hockey, football and baseball with other kids in the neighborhood. There are no referees or umpires. We just have fun.

I have many friends of my own, some popular and some not so popular. I make new friends but keep the old. I sometimes ponder my future—what I will do later in life. I dream big. As a scientist, I'll find a cure for cancer. As a politician, I'll end war and starvation. As an author, I'll write a novel and bring encouragement to others. I carry the burdens of the world as my own. Moreover, I believe I can change the world—make it better. I feel a sense of responsibility. God's put me here for a reason. I must take what God's given me, pray to Him for direction, and find some way to make His world a better place. My childhood dreams are grandiose and idyllic. And I chase those dreams. With God's help, all things are possible.

In 1970, Dad resigns his post as engineer at General Electric. I overhear his conversations with Mom. He tells her he's tired of working for others. He says he wants to start a business of his own. In the end, he does just that. He works as a self-employed family historian, as an investor, and as a stay-at-home dad. Mom finds new employment as a full-time teacher at Proctor Elementary School in Topsfield.

Dad is a good man, and he does his best to shepherd me, his eight-year-old son. I hear his direction countless times: "Do as I say not as I do, honor thy parents, the world doesn't revolve around you, Chris." He often ends his conversations with me with a lesson—full of thou's, and should's and ought's. We talk about religion and the Parable of the Sower.

"Hear the Word, Chris—it will serve you for the rest of your life."

Dad tells me not to put myself first—but to think always of the greater good. He encourages me to do my best in everything I do. His words resonate within me and I push myself all the more. His favorite saying is "Honesty is the best policy." He says he simply wants what's best for me and my brothers and the family. And I believe him and most everything he says. After all he is my father.

I'm more serious than most boys in my class in junior high school. I occasionally feel picked upon—sometimes even among friends and family. I keep to myself for fear of saying too much, or simply saying the wrong thing. Dad says I'm too sensitive—that I need to let the water rush off my back. Mom urges me to simply ask a question now and then. Maybe there's something wrong with me. But no—God has a plan for me and I'm determined to succeed. Someday if I work hard and pray enough all of my efforts will pay off. Somehow, I will make a difference in this world with His help.

With encouragement from my parents, I study long hours each evening during high school. I'm good at Math and Science, but I love to write stories. I write stories for English classes at school. I also write stories in my spare time. I take Advanced Placement classes in almost every subject. At school many of my teachers tell me I'm just like my older brothers: "You're another one of the Holdstrom boys who always try hard and are good kids." I also hear it at home from my father: "Like your brothers you are a Holdstrom—so be strong and proud of your heritage—and act like a man." I get good grades in school and I'm a good athlete. But I sometimes wonder if I live up to these expectations—am I really as good as Dad and my teachers say? Or did my brothers simply pave the way before me?

I take a class in Computer Science during my junior year in high school. I'm good at writing programs early on in the semester. But I'm challenged by more complicated assignments toward the end of the course. I collaborate with others on some programs, study hard for written class exams, and easily pass the course with a "B". At times I wonder if I earned that grade. Is it fair to collaborate with others? But I did work hard, I did ace the final exam, and I learned a great deal about computer logic through the experience.

I run the 2-mile, the mile, and the half-mile on the high school track team. I'm a good distance runner. I often place among the top three competitors each time I race. But my passion is soccer. I play soccer year-round. I'm a defender. Being a star forward or midfielder has never been my ambition. I prefer to be in the background—sizing up my opponent and preventing the other team from scoring. I make the varsity soccer team my sophomore, junior, and senior years in high school. But do I earn my varsity letters on the soccer and track teams? Or do I receive the letters just because I'm a Holdstrom?

I attend a party with friends one evening the summer before my senior year. For the first time in my life, I drink too much beer. But I have fun just hanging out with friends. I feel like I'm gaining independence from my father—in fact, I'm still a child. A girl I'd known since grade school, Suzie, comes up to me at the end of the party and kisses me on the lips. Her kiss is soft against my dry chapped lips. It feels good, but I am very drunk. Never before had I been kissed on the lips. Never before had a girl shown any interest in me whatsoever—let alone one of the most popular girls in our high school class. I walk home that night on the quiet backroads of Topsfield, hiding in the shadows as cars pass by. I don't want to be seen drunk. Moreover, I don't want my father to know that I've been drinking. I stagger home—roughly two miles. I'm sick that night and through the next morning. But Dad and Mom suspect nothing.

I sit nervously waiting to take my SATs one Saturday morning in October. I'd celebrated my seventeenth birthday just a few weeks before. There is almost total silence in the school cafeteria as students take their seats and fill in their names on the exam sheet bubbles. Mr. Dussault, the principal of the high school walks briskly into the cafeteria and stands before us: "Boys and girls, I have some terrible news. Four of your classmates were involved in a horrible car accident last night."

They got in a truck and drove towards Georgetown, just a few miles from my home. One headlight working, the car veered off the road and into a tree. Three survived. That same girl who two months ago kissed me at a party—a friend who I'd known since kindergarten—lost her life. There is no one to blame. Suzie is gone…To a better place for sure…But gone.

The exam starts thirty minutes late. No test ever seemed more trivial. I hear the quiet sobs of students around me as the exam period begins. A few students refuse to take the test. They can't escape the sudden loss. They walk away. I look down at the hundreds of perfect ovals on my SAT exam sheet. We square-danced together as kids in grade school…I taught her how to add, subtract, multiply and divide—she helped me laugh…I hear her innocent giggle…I see her brilliant smile We danced and swayed to the sounds of rock 'n roll music in the high school gym just last week…She's not gone…She can't be.

Focus on the test questions. SATs, college, career—it all seems trivial. No matter how hard I pray or what scores I get on my SATs or what college I attend or what career I pursue—she's gone, and nothing can change that. I complete the entire Math section but leave much of the Verbal unanswered. My hopes and plans have run amuck. I'm not going Ivy League. Not after this test.

Her funeral service is held downtown at St. Rose Church. Almost all of the Class of 1980 prays for her. Most all of us will go on to graduate, but I am stuck. Suzie has no future. I've lost a friend for the first time in my life and there's nothing I can do about it. I'm angry at the world. I didn't ask for this. God hears my self-pity and anguish. He is silent. I tell God to go to Hell. And that's precisely where He would send me.

Chapter 2 | **Without a Net**

A few friends call me Dr. Holdstrom during my senior year in high school. They think I have what it takes to make it as a doctor. I guess I think I do, too. I'll make good money. I'll have a family. I'll help others with their ailments—their disabilities—maybe even save some lives.

I gain confidence. I apply to four colleges that winter. Brown University is my first choice. I'm a good student, an Eagle Scout, and a Boston Globe All-Scholastic Soccer player. I'm competitive. I always do my best. As a high school student, I may not be the very brightest in my class—but I am diligent about my studies. As an Eagle Scout I'm physically strong, mentally awake, and morally straight. But am I competent enough to make it as a student in the Ivy League? Friends from high school say, "Go for it, Holdstrom," or "You the man." By April, I receive acceptances from all four schools.

When the mailing from Brown arrives, I tear it open and read the cover letter out loud. With each sentence I read there is pride—this acceptance will make me the envy of all of my friends at school. My plans and prayers have been realized. My career ambitions are starting to unfold much as I had dreamt. I will study hard, earn my degrees and pursue a career in medicine—dedicated to helping others who are sick and less fortunate. This is God's plan for me. This is my dream.

"Congratulations." Dad looks up from his work, shuffles some papers, claps his hands once, and smiles.

"You know, Chris, this is a great honor and you should feel proud about all of your acceptances. But I'm not sure we can afford to send you to a school like Brown. Your older brothers went to less expensive public universities. We have to be fair with them. Right? Just remember this, Chris. Whatever you do in this life, it's not where you go, it's what you do while you're there."

The smile on my face falls deep to the pit of my stomach. Brown has been my goal for the past year. This is my plan. There is no alternative. In the weeks that follow, I often talk with Dad about Brown and my career ambitions. In the end, my parents let me chase my dream. They agree to pay nearly all of the expense of my freshman year. Beyond that nothing is certain. I tell Dad I'll earn scholarships from my sophomore year going forward. I can stand on my own. After all, I am a Holdstrom.

I receive several honors and local scholarships at my high school graduation. Everything seems to go my way. I focus more time on myself and my future. I feel almost infallible. My career goals and ambitions, my commitment to God to somehow make the world a better place…I have to be a straight-A student at Brown. I have to be a standout student athlete. I have to be accepted by a top medical school. I have to make lots of new friends along the way. I want to do some good in the world. I want to do something to help those less fortunate. But my plans and ambitions center around me—and what I want. I pray to God for direction and blessing. God is silent.

It is my freshman year at Brown University. I just turned 18 years old. Now I'm a man. I study hard during the week, and I practice with the freshman soccer team. On the weekends I party and sing and joke with friends. We have fun. We drink beer and wine. We sing and shout to the sounds of the Doors and Springsteen. But something is missing. Sometimes I'm a man of God. I pray often as I lie awake in bed at night. But mostly, I'm not right.

There are challenging classes in calculus, biology, and chemistry. But computer science is my downfall. In January and February—I receive high marks. My programs are crisp and efficient. But programming assignments are taking more and more time from my pre-med classes. My grades in calculus and biology start to slip. Maybe I'm not good enough. Maybe I'm not cut out to be a doctor. Winter turns to spring. I continue to lose confidence. It's too late in the semester to drop the computer science class. The deadline has long since passed. I feel anything but infallible. I envision failure—my plan to pursue a career in medicine slipping away. Periodic fears twist and distort my thoughts—hindering my ability to concentrate.

No longer can I focus on studies without becoming ensnarled in anxiety. This last program—I can't figure it out. And the assignments—each program is more challenging—more complex than the one before it…If I fail, I'll never make it into med school. I may never amount to much of anything. I'm trapped…And all the money my parents are spending. Is there no way out? Help me God, please help.

The programming language, Pascal, is logical—but I am not. Professor Wilson calls me into his office one morning in April. "Chris, the last program you turned in was not your own, was it." I know he is right. He knows he is right. A rush of fear and self-pity floods my mind. I shut down. I can't talk. I nod and cry out self-loathingly. I've broken all the rules I believe in. I'm dishonest. I did my worst. I'm my own worst enemy. I'm battered, embarrassed, and humbled. I've let myself down. I've let everyone down. I've failed my family. I've failed my friends. My greatest fears are realized... I am a failure.

My final grade for computer science is no credit. I won't be going to medical school now. My career as a doctor helping others is over—before it's even started. Failure is a temporary mark on my school record. It's a more permanent stain on my conscience. My only comfort is prayer. I'm bankrupt in everyone's eyes but His. But this is my own doing. I can't blame anyone but me—and I can't forgive myself. That once sensitive boy who should not cry has grown to be a man. And I weep. I am a disgrace. I don't know where to turn. I call Dad later that afternoon. I fear his reaction more than death itself.

"Chris, it's easy to get into trouble. We've all made mistakes. Just remember this—your mom and I, and your brothers too, we all love you and we're here to help you in any way we can. I can tell you're upset. This may seem like some huge, catastrophic trial right now but in the long run this is nothing. I guess at your age I'd have seen this whole thing as a crisis too. But don't be so hard on yourself. Believe me, this is nothing. Learn from your mistake and go on. It's a long life…Now tell me what I can do. Should I drive down to see you? I can be there in three hours."

In the end, Dad drives down to Providence and rescues me in my anguish. Dad comforts and guides me. He encourages me to tell no one about my recent fiasco. "After all Chris, no one would understand…And no one really gives a damn anyway." Maybe Dad is right.

I tell no one else about my folly. I am too ashamed and humiliated to share the burden with friends, my brothers, or even my mom.

I complete the semester and get passing grades in my other courses, but my career ambitions are dashed. I'm not going to medical school, not after this failure. No medical school would have anything to do with me in my deceit.

That summer I work at a machine shop a few miles from home. I'm not a machinist by trade but I've picked up enough skills on the job the past summer to earn my hourly wage. Each week I put in forty hours plus overtime. I bank as much money as I can for what will be my sophomore year at Brown. The workdays are long. The smell of burning machine oil, the smoke, the monotony—I count each minute. Plans for a career in medicine are behind me, but I'm going back to Brown. My sophomore year will be different. I'm invited back to school early to try out for the varsity soccer team. I'll redeem my mistakes in the classroom. I'll refocus my career ambitions. I'll earn my degree.

I return to Brown in August. Little has changed—failures from my freshman year haunt my conscience. I had a chance to fulfil my dream. I let it slip—all due to my own futility. I cheated and I got what I deserved. I'm a failure and an idiot—the ultimate fool. I fail at everything I do. At the same time, I want to be nobody's fool. After all, I am a Holdstrom. I can't forgive myself for my blunder. I can't see why anyone would. Anxiety runs through my veins like ice water. Am I smart enough to succeed at a school like Brown? No. Do I deserve to be here? No. Can my parents afford to send me to a school as expensive as Brown? No. What if I fail again? Disaster.

Anxiety and panic lead to sleeplessness at night. I lie awake in bed worrying about my future. What am I doing here? Where do I belong? Where am I headed? I have no plan...

I nearly pick a fight with a friend from the varsity soccer team one afternoon at practice. The next day during a scrimmage I tackle the ball from the most prolific goal scorer on our squad. The ball shoots straight up thirty feet into the clear blue autumn sky, before falling back to the turf between us. The striker grabs his ankle, grimaces in pain and disbelief, and falls to his knees. His ankle is fractured. I have broken the ankle of the best player on our team. There is silence. Every mouth is aghast, all eyes are fixed upon me. The striker cries out in pain, but I feel nothing--no pain or remorse. Coach calls out to me in his gruff, New England accent. "Holdstrom, what have you done?"

"I'm sorry," I reply under my breath. There is nothing more to say. I sprint from the pitch and run all the way to my dorm room across campus. I throw myself down on my bed and try to console my troubled conscience. I've cost the team it's best player. I'm unworthy of playing soccer at this level. I'm unworthy of being a student at this school. Where do I belong? I don't belong here. I quit the team the next day.

The downslide continues. I go without sleep most nights. I am fogged and confused. I cannot think. I cannot break the stupor. The world goes on about me but I am no longer part of the world. Friends at Brown watch as I gradually slip from reality. At first, they think I'm just joking around, but I am not. I become more aloof, seemingly catatonic. When my friends talk and try to help me, I am focused within—deaf to their words.

I stop eating. Lack of sustenance compounds the chaos. Ideas cast rampantly about my brain without check. Transient thoughts connect in bizarre and delusional ways. I can no longer control my thoughts. There is no way to stop the debacle. I feel all powerful one moment. The next moment I am frail and exhausted.

My friends Brian and Bill walk beside me. They lead me to University Health Services on a Saturday morning. I am weak and delirious—beyond exhaustion. The doctor sees me for ten minutes. I say nothing. I am dazed. Weak, weaker, failing, failed. I am not who I was. Never again will I know that person.

My father arrives within a few hours. Dad has come to my rescue. He drives me home to Topsfield. My mind is wired—beyond alert. Every noise sparks fear and anxiety. The furnace rumbling in the basement of our home—a bomb about to detonate. Articles in the local paper—either I'm the toast of all Topsfield, or a loathsome menace. I am beyond exhaustion. My mind has imploded. My thoughts spiral out of control. "Chris, you have to get some sleep." Dad grabs me by the shoulders and directs me down the hall to my bedroom. I lie awake in bed until dawn.

That morning we drive to Proctor School where Mom teaches second grade. I'm restless and agitated. I can't sit still for more than a few seconds. As Dad drives me home, I grab the steering wheel, turn off the ignition, and swerve the car to the side of the road. I open the door, step from the Ford Escort and walk back toward the center of town, the direction from which we came. Dad follows behind me in the car. He wants to help. He tries to help. But there's nothing he can say. I'm at odds with him. I'm deaf to his words. My focus is within. Dad notifies the police and asks for their assistance.

I walk aimlessly about Topsfield for several hours—confused, dehydrated and sleepless. Two police officers find me kneeling outside St. Rose Church. I'm powerful and wise one moment—I am weak and dead to the world the next. The officers pull me to my feet and sit me in the back of a cruiser, the door locked behind me. My mind turns wildly. I am mighty yet frail. I am fearless yet afraid. I cry out in anguish. I beg for mercy. My prayers are answered but not as I expected.

They drive me to Danvers State Hospital, a mental health facility the next town over. I'm seen briefly by a doctor and strapped to a stretcher. I feel the pinch of a needle—a dull ache in my left shoulder. My thoughts turn and twist—beyond comprehension. I fear for my life. I struggle frantically to free myself from the straps that bind me. But it's no use. The strength in my arms and legs abate—my head and neck heave against the stretcher as I'm lifted into an ambulance. I am trapped—at the mercy of those around me. "Let me out of here!" I plead. I feel the ambulance surge as the driver turns the ignition. I hear the shrill of the siren all about me. Oh Lord, God Almighty... What have I done? Where are you taking me? My mind drifts into oblivion. I abruptly pass out.

Chapter 3 | Without Hope

A breakfast tray lies on the floor next to the door. Soggy Corn Flakes, cold scrambled eggs, stale toast. I eat voraciously. I hear a key rasp and click in lock…the door creaks open behind me.

"Good morning, Christopher. My name is Dr. Stabler. How do you feel?"

A man short in stature stands in the threshold. The accent is incontestably Boston. His voice is shallow and rough. He is neatly dressed in a tan corduroy suit, white shirt and brown tie. Black horn-rimmed glasses lay across his face. His complexion is ruddy, veiled behind a well-groomed graying moustache and beard.

"Do you know what day it is, Christopher? It's Friday, October 23, 1981. You're in the hospital—Addison Gilbert Hospital—Walker II, the psychiatric ward. You've been with us about a week though you probably don't realize it…I see you've done some writing on the walls. Well, that's alright—we need to paint this room anyway.

"I'm afraid I have some bad news to share with you this morning, Christopher. Do you recall meeting Dr. Stoughton last week? He was your doctor. I'm afraid Dr. Stoughton died in a horrible car accident the other night. I am sorry. I realize the two of you met only once. You may not remember meeting him—you were in quite a stupor at the time. So going forward—so long as you're here on this unit—I will be your doctor."

There's a lull in his speech as if to invite conversation. I have nothing to say. I feel dizzy and faint from the medicines.

"Christopher, we need to talk. Let's think this through together…You were at Brown. You lost control. You had a psychotic episode. Do you know what that is? Well, it could have been the result of a chemical imbalance or mood swing…or perhaps something else. Tell me, Christopher, have you ever taken drugs?"

"No sir, never—only beer and wine."

"I want you to think about this, Christopher. When you were at Brown, could someone have slipped something into your drink at a party? You don't have to answer this question now, but think about it. We had to medicate you heavily to bring you down. For awhile, we thought we'd lost you. Do you remember the straightjacket we put you in the other night? Christopher, you broke out of that straightjacket. We had to throw it away.

"You're going to be with us awhile. At least a few weeks, maybe longer. But don't worry, your father called the insurance company. You're covered for a month. So just concentrate on getting better. That's all you have to do now. You'll be on some different meds over the next week or two—until we find the regimen that works best for you. Don't fight their effects. Let the meds work for you.

"We're going to let you out of your room today, Christopher, but gradually. I want you to meet the other patients and to get to know them. You don't have to be their best friend but you do need to talk and be part of the program—you will learn from others and others will learn from you. While you're here you will be busy. We want you to stay out of your room as much as possible, but if ever you feel the least bit anxious or uncomfortable, I want you to return right here to this room. Understand?"

I want to go home. Walker II is not my home. There's no place to hide. Patients pace the hallways, some sob and cry incessantly. Others yell and shout and fight among themselves. Doctors and nurses and counselors are everywhere.

"You look a little tense today, Christopher. How do you feel?"

"I feel fine. I just want to get back to school. I don't belong here!"

Weekdays are slow. We have meetings most every hour each weekday. Patients talk about their relationships with friends and family. The talk is usually about a parent or spouse who is physically or verbally abusive. I don't talk much—I usually sit quietly. I don't have a troubled past. I don't know why I'm here. I don't know how I got sick. I question whether I was ever really sick to begin with. I speak only when spoken to—and there's not much to say. I'm ready to get on with my life.

Three days a week we do arts and crafts. We finish small pieces of pottery and woodwork. We draw and paint. Some patients create ugly and violent stories through their creations. I draw my future, crawling out of this pit. Climbing out. Getting on with life. I need to get back to school. My future…There must be something more.

Dr. Stabler meets with me daily. "Slow down, Christopher. You just got here three weeks ago. Do I need to remind you how sick you were when you came to us? Do you remember how sick you were then? You were very sick, Christopher. You were reeling and you couldn't slow down. We had to bring you down with meds—remember? Give the medicines some time. We don't want you to have a relapse. We need to check your Lithium levels and make sure they're stable. That could take a few weeks. You will also need to come down some off the Haldol. All these things take time. But for now, work with the other patients. You're spending far too much time alone in your room. We need to be sure you're ready before you leave."

Weekends are hell. Nothing to do but sit and watch TV. I can't read—my vision is blurred by the Haldol. There is no place to go. Dad and Mom visit me for an hour each weekend. I tell Dad I want to go home. "Not today, Chris. Dr. Stabler says it's not time yet." And I hate my predicament all the more. Why me, God? Why?

On my twenty-fifth day of confinement, I work through a battery of tests with Elaine, the hospital psychologist. Elaine shows me a series of two-dimensional diagrams. For each diagram, Elaine points to an array of drawings from which I am to identify the same figure in three dimensions. I focus in turn on each of the diagrams. They revolve into three-dimensional images before my eyes.

Dr. Stabler opens the door and asks to speak with me. "Christopher, I apologize for interrupting your meeting with Elaine but we've come to a very important decision. I need to discuss this with you before I leave for the weekend. Simply put— you need more time here on Walker II, more than the thirty days we had planned on. You're not talking enough with the other patients and you rarely participate in meetings. You have a condition called bipolar affective disorder. Some call it manic depression. A little extra time will assure all of us that you're ready to return home. I've talked with your parents. Your father signed the paperwork—you'll be a ward of the state. Now don't worry— that may sound like a bad thing, but I promise that you won't be here more than an additional week or two. This is all for the best, Christopher—for you and your parents. I can assure you that."

My worst fear has been realized. I am stuck in this place for God knows how long. Fear turns to frustration—and frustration turns to anger. I don't belong here. Will I ever be free of this place? I have no life. I have no freedom. I have been betrayed by my father. I have lost everything. And I weep.

Hope. Annie paces the hallways and often mumbles in rhymes. Annie's in her mid-thirties, tall and of slight build. Her face is pale and gaunt and her sandy blonde hair falls flat to her shoulders. Annie's troubled like most all patients on the ward. One Sunday afternoon in November, Annie disappears. None of the staff notice Annie's absence until it's too late. She is gone, free, completely rid of this place. Dr. Stabler arrives on the scene and calls an emergency meeting within minutes. "This is a very grave situation. Annie needs help. She's not going to make it on her own without her medicines." Dr. Stabler is clearly upset with his staff. But he's more concerned for his lost sheep. Did Annie make it on her own? I never again heard her name mentioned. Annie has something I long for. Annie is free.

Day 40. I'm to be released from the hospital this afternoon—no longer a "ward" of the state. My diagnosis at discharge is type 1 bipolar affective disorder. I say goodbyes to most of the patients, nurses, and counselors. They all politely wish me luck. My father arrives at three o'clock. I quickly grab a plastic garbage bag full of my belongings and head for the exit. The lock releases. My father holds the door open before me. I feel strangely vulnerable as I depart Walker II. I'm free from the shelter. My dad has come to my rescue. Now I must prove myself in the real world. That worry fades as Dad and I cross the hospital parking lot. God be with me—I will start anew. This is my time. I feel free...

Living at home during the holidays is a burden. Friends visit me and my parents at our home in Topsfield. They talk about their successes at work and at school while I fester in my failures. Everyone is jovial but me. My parents tell friends and neighbors that mononucleosis led to my recent departure from Brown. Dad may be right for concealing my true diagnosis from others. "After all Chris, no one would understand...And no one really gives a damn anyway." But I feel as though I'm living a lie. I've learned to hate the hospital. And I hate the fact that my father kept me there all of those weeks.

As the holidays pass, Dr. Stabler urges my parents not to let me return to school right away. He recommends that I participate in an outpatient day program. I'm out of the hospital, still unable to do as I choose. My emotions dip. I fall further—frustrated, anguished, and depressed. Dear Lord, how could this happen? I'm nineteen years old. The doctors say I'm mentally ill? How could this be? I should be at school—writing papers—studying for exams. Instead I'm here at home with my parents. Why can't I be like my friends? I need to get back to Brown—where I should be. I'm losing precious time...

In March, I return to work at the local machine shop. The work doesn't interest me. I am not very adept at building custom machine parts. I work the drill press, de-bur parts, and clean machines—counting the weeks until I return to school. I do a lot of thinking each day at work. I think as I run the streets of Topsfield each evening. I pray as I lie awake in bed most nights. When I think about Brown—I feel battered and embarrassed. Moreover, I have no plan. How can I justify the expense of a school like Brown when I have no plan for my future? I submit an application to transfer to the University of Massachusetts at Amherst. The thought is comforting. My older brother graduated from UMass. My education will be far less expense as an in-state student. This will be my new beginning. In April, I'm admitted to UMass as a sophomore.

Mom and Dad drive me to Amherst for fall semester orientation that August. I live in a dorm suite with three guys on the north side of campus. As the semester begins, I attend classes during the day and drink beer with my new-found friends at night—all to be part of the group. I feel like an adult, but I am still a child. None of my new friends know that I was recently hospitalized with bipolar disorder. None of these friends know that I take Lithium Carbonate and Haldol.

I begin to question my need for the medicines. I'm on my own, doing well, making new friends. Do I really need the Lithium Carbonate and Haldol? What do the meds do anyway? No one really knows what they do. And the side effects—I have to pee every hour of the day and night, my hands tremble constantly, and there's the risk of kidney failure and tardive dyskinesia over time. I don't need the medicines. I may get very sick or perhaps even die if the beer and Haldol interact.

I stop taking Haldol in early September. Drinking beer further impairs my judgment. I'm still haunted by my failures at Brown. Moreover, I'm fearful of my future. I have no idea what I want to do with my life. I have no plan. Without the Haldol, I sleep fewer hours with each passing night until I stop sleeping altogether. Sleeplessness turns to irrationality, and in my stupor, I stop taking Lithium Carbonate. I eat less with each passing day, until I stop eating altogether. Lack of sleep and lack of sustenance, I fall further—bizarre thoughts run amok about my brain. One moment, I'm a prophet—wise and omnipotent. The next moment, I am shunned—the weakest of fools.

A friend from my hometown—a fellow student at UMass—stops by my dorm room. It's been three weeks since I've taken meds. I'm not right. My thoughts revolve—quickly and randomly. My mind cannot keep pace. Vile slurs skip from my tongue. My friend Kate and I talk for less than a minute—long enough for her to realize that I've gone mad. She jumps abruptly to her feet and runs from the dorm suite—afraid and confused as to what's gotten into Chris.

Dazed and delirious—I walk through the fog to University Health Services the next day—escorted by one of my suitemates. The doctor sees me briefly. My father arrives and rescues me in my stupor.

"What happened, Chris?"

"Amherst…dam burst…Amherst…dam burst…Amherst…dam burst…"

My father drives me home to Topsfield that afternoon. I am past exhaustion. I lie down in bed. I cannot sleep. My brain is wired—beyond alert. The next morning, I slip out the front door at sunrise—before my parents notice that I'm gone. I walk about Topsfield for hours. I have gone on a walkabout. By dusk, I'm dehydrated and hallucinating. I am all powerful one moment. I'm buried in a barrage of voices the next. My older brother finds me walking along Ipswich Road the next town over from Topsfield. He leads me back to the car. I laugh and sing and play all the way to Walker II. I see Dad smile in the rear-view mirror. "I don't know what he's got, but whatever he's got, he's got it bad."

Back on medicines at Walker II, my thoughts gradually decelerate. I know who I am and I know where I am. I'm in a safe place. But my Lithium level is very low. It's going to take a few weeks to correct this. I need to talk with counselors, nurses, and the other patients. I need to participate in meetings and activities.

I need to stay out of my room as much as possible. My mood stabilizes. But I have no patience—not with Dr. Stabler, not with my parents, not with God. Oh Lord, why me? Why am I going through this? I should be at school. Maybe I was sick before, but I'm better now. I don't belong here. My friends are all in college. I should be there, too…

I leave the hospital after thirty days. Only immediate family and a few of our closest friends know the true circumstances behind my recent misfortune. All others are told I had a relapse of mononucleosis. I'm ashamed of my illness. I'm ashamed of myself. I fall headlong into despair and depression. The mental anguish is incapacitating—I go to bed before nine o'clock most nights—I have trouble getting out of bed before ten o'clock most mornings. Taking my life is not an option—Mom taught me that at a young age. Dad tells me time and again, "Your mom and I—we're proud of who you are."

"For what?" I retort. I feel like the black sheep of the family. "Dad, do you love me?"

"Yes, I love you, Son. And your mom does, too. You're our son. We love you more than anything. And your brothers do, too."

"Dad, I feel awful. Look at me—I'm not in school. I have no job. I have no plan for my life. I'm nothing…"

"Don't say that, Chris. We love you very much…Remember when you were in high school—all the honors and awards you received at graduation. Life isn't always that way, Chris. Life can be hard on a person. I love you just as much now as I loved you then… Think of it this way. God has thrown you a curve ball. It doesn't really matter what you do in this lifetime—whether you strike out or hit a home run. You're still my son. I will love you forever."

"Do you really love me, Dad—even now when I'm so depressed I could die?"

And Dad wept. I'd never seen him cry before that day—nor would I ever see him shed a tear again.

"Chris, I love you…You're going through a tough time right now. I know it. Your mom knows it. Dr. Stabler knows it. But it doesn't have to be like this…and it won't be for long. Sure, things seem dark right now. But it will get better. You're young. You have your whole life ahead of you. Don't give up. Don't be a quitter. Your mom and I—we love you…and we're proud of who you are…"

Come February, I start work again at the local machine shop. In the months that follow my work responsibilities increase. I'm asked to keep watch over the automated machinery—machines that mill and drill with precision at the touch of a button. One day as I watch over one of these Goliaths—the head of the machine crashes to the steel bed below with a thunderous roar. A metal fragment, two inches in diameter, snaps from the drill bit and soars past me in a blur—within a few feet of my right shoulder. The fragment crashes against a smaller machine beside me—leaving a three-inch dent in its wake. I look at the one machine frozen in place—embedded in the steel plate below it. Milky coolant flows and spills over the bed of the machine. I turn and face the dented machinery to my right. Lord knows, I don't belong here.

I pray most nights as I lie awake in bed—I ask God for hope and direction. Sometimes I'm a man, but most of the time I'm still a child. I want out of the machine shop. I want to get on with my life. I want to get on with my schooling. And I want it all—now. I dream of a time when I will no longer be the patient—when I will have the freedom to make decisions for myself. I'll have a wife and three kids. I'll live the American dream and be happy. My life will be perfect and I will be the perfect husband and father… If only it were that easy.

I meet with Dr. Stabler on a weekly basis that spring. I don't talk much during therapy. Dad tells me not to talk about the family and there's not much to say. I usually sit quietly—focused more on the rhythmic ticking of the wall clock than the words of my doctor—waiting for therapy to end. I take my medicines as prescribed. I work at the machine shop Monday through Saturday.

I am frustrated with the meds, and suffocated by their side effects. They deter me and thwart my ambitions.

At Dr. Stabler's suggestion—I take a class that spring—a night class in accounting at Salem State College. I'm not particularly motivated by the subject, but I do well on the mid-term and final exams. It feels good to excel. I am capable of much more. Dr. Stabler encourages me to attend summer session at UMass before I take classes there as a full-time student in the fall. I enroll in a writing composition class—a required course for all undergraduates.

As a final assignment for the course, I write a story about Walker II. Not a detailed account but more a collection of my thoughts and impressions—an abstract of my experience. I spend hours trying to capture my thoughts and emotions on paper. I write about mania and the subsequent frustrations of being hospitalized—the anguish and depression—a story true to my sense of loss, helplessness, and humility. I complete the seven-page paper and feel a sense of accomplishment and relief. A few weeks later, I stop by Walker II and share copies of the paper with several of my former counselors. The counselors thank me for the paper. I stop by Dr. Stabler's office. He's in a meeting. I leave a copy of the story for him under his office door.

As a sophomore at UMass, I create an independent study focused on health policy and management. I work at a YMCA camp in Northampton as a senior counselor the following summer. For the first summer in five years, I am free from the oil, the smoke and the clamour of the machine shop.

I submit an application that fall to intern at the World Health Organization in Geneva, Switzerland. My application is accepted. I live in a dorm suite at the Centre Universitaire Geneve from June through August the following summer. It is an awesome experience. As an intern I research and document a meta-analysis on control of the parasitic disease Schistosomiasis. As a tourist I visit many cities and towns across Switzerland, and parts of France and southern Germany. On the plane flight from Geneva back to

Boston, I denounce my need for the medicines. I've worked and lived abroad on my own. The side effects of the meds are not just a burden—they set me apart—a constant reminder of my recent failures. As the plane touches down at Logan Airport I declare myself free of the bipolar condition. I stop taking my daily regimen of Lithium Carbonate and Haldol, and for awhile, I feel free.

I return to UMass that September—without meds, and to a lesser extent free of their side effects. I'm enrolled in three graduate level classes. I lie awake in bed most nights thinking about studies. Without medicines, I sleep less and less each night. Over the course of several days, my thoughts obscure—I stop attending classes and I soon stop eating. Lack of sleep and lack of sustenance—my thoughts turn dark and delusional. No one understands me. Some are out to get me... I am a genius–a prodigy. I can save the world from its miseries... Doesn't anyone understand?

Bizarre thoughts race and twist about my brain until my disability within spills over. Crazed words that frantically ruminate within me skip randomly from my tongue. My roommates, Danny and Mark, don't know of my condition or of my need for medicine, but something is clearly wrong. Danny calls my parents. My father arrives within a few hours.

The next day I land at Walker II. Back on medicines, my mood calms within a few days. My thoughts decelerate—the grandiose notions subside. I'm in a safe place. But my Lithium level is low... It's going to take a few weeks to correct this. I need to talk with counselors, nurses and the other patients...I need to participate in meetings and activities. I need to stay out of my room as much as possible...

As my Lithium level stabilizes, I soon lose patience. Dear Lord, why am I here? Yes, I was sick. But I'm not sick now... For the first time since being diagnosed with bipolar disorder, I acknowledge to Dr. Stabler, my parents and myself that I must stay on all of my medicines. "There is no alternative."

| # Without a Compass

I see Dr. Stabler for weekly therapy and medication management after being discharged from Walker II in October. Dr. Stabler and my father remind me countless times that I must stay on my meds. I'm an adult. I'm twenty-three years old. I don't need their direction…I take my medicines as prescribed each morning when I awake and each night before going to bed. I write my undergraduate thesis by day. I dream at night about my future career as a healthcare professional helping others. And I pray to God that He might carry me in that direction.

"Christopher, you've been seeing me since you first came to Walker II almost four years ago. You've met with me for a half hour or more each week for much of that time. I've learned a lot about you since we first met, Christopher. Sure, you're smart and good looking—whether you admit it or not. And you have nearly perfect auditory recall; that is, when you listen. Yet for all the years I've known you, you're still very quiet. You hardly say much of anything.

"You may not believe me, Christopher—but as I've told you many times before you do have an illness. Some call it manic depression, but I think you're more depressed than bipolar. You still have doubts about whether therapy can help you. But this is not a sham. I—Phillip Stabler—have helped hundreds of patients like you over the years—many of whom had no place else to turn.

"Now Christopher, before we start today's therapy, I want you to think back for a few minutes to a story you wrote two years ago at UMass. You wrote a paper about your experiences on Walker II, and you shared that story with me and my staff.

"Christopher, that paper was distorted and repulsive. It should never have been written—let alone shared with others. You made me, your father and my entire team of counselors and therapists sound like a bunch of heartless, callous buffoons. How could you write such hurtful and destructive words about people who cared for you and did so much to try and help you?

"Christopher, I hold all of my patients—including you—as my ultimate meaning and focus in life. It's what I do. It's who I am. In your paper, you went so far as to proclaim the disappearance of one of my patients on the unit as a comforting and reassuring event. Christopher—that patient who disappeared two years ago has never been heard of again. Not by me, not by my staff, not by her family and loved ones…You don't think that hangs over me and gnaws at me every day?

"Now I realize you may not have meant any harm, but in sharing that paper with my team you caused me pain—a lot of pain. The content of your paper was more than disruptive. It caused a rift between me and my staff, Christopher—a rift that's torn Walker II to pieces ever since. Some of the best and most trusted members of my team have left me—disturbed largely by the disparaging content of that paper. It took many years for me to assemble that team, Christopher. Some of the best counselors that ever worked for me were part of that group. Most of them have resigned now. They're gone and they won't be coming back. In effect, your paper has been a primary cog in the decimation of my team, Christopher…and I hold you accountable.

"So, for the next half hour you and I are going to try something different—a different kind of therapy. Something that will require some imagination—a type of hypnosis. You wrote a story about Walker II and shared it with me and my staff. Now allow me to turn the tables. This afternoon I am going to tell you a story—a story about you. My story may cause you some pain, Christopher—and if so, I am not sorry. Consider any pain you may experience from this afternoon's therapy—an eye for an eye—for all the struggles you've put me through these past months. For the most part you have a good life, Christopher—but like all of us you experience some difficult times, too. Think of it this way, Christopher. I'm not trying to harm or scare you. I'm trying to help you prepare for those times.

"First, there's something I want to show you. I don't usually share this with my clients, Christopher—but in your case I'll make an exception. In this tiny wooden box, I keep a small diamond pendant. Let me show it to you—see how the diamond sparkles in this light? To start with I want you to just sit back, rest comfortably in your chair, take a deep breath and relax…I'm going to dangle this diamond pendant before you on this chain like this…I want you to put all of your focus on the pendant…See how the diamond sparkles as I twirl it before you in this light… Focus only on the stone…That's it…Good…

"Now as you maintain focus on the diamond, I want you slowly—ever so slowly—to close your eyes. That's it… Good… Though your eyelids are closed, you do not fall asleep. You hear every word I say… Now I want you to concentrate on each breath that you take. Feel your chest rise and fall as you breathe. Picture it in your mind Good… You're doing much better, Christopher. You seem much more relaxed…

"Now, I'm going to tell you a story. You will hear every word I speak. But you will do more than hear my words. You will picture each event in your mind…

"Over the coming years, you continue to have illnesses much like the one that brought you here to me. Yes, you see I was right—you have got something…You see, most people don't think like you, Christopher. You think on many different levels—all at once. The medicines I prescribe for you—the Lithium Carbonate and Haldol—they help you to stay on one level at a time. Oh, you do a pretty good job of taking your medicines most of the time, but certain times of the year you have trouble. The illnesses deter you—and your medicines need adjusting from time to time—but the disruptions don't stop you. You are very determined in school and in everything you do…And while on your medicines, you're capable of great things. Oh, I know you believe the meds slow you down, and they do somewhat, but in fact they help you to think more clearly. Keep this one thing in mind, Christopher—you must stay on your medicines.

"But let's continue with your story…A few years pass. Oh Christopher, someone very close to you dies. I would think you'd be more upset. But I shouldn't comment on that. How you react to the death of a loved one is your business. You speak at the funeral service. You carry the coffin.

"Several years later... You live in a southern city. You have a girlfriend with dark skin. This friend of yours went to all the right schools alright but she's not right for you. Your friendship with her lasts awhile. And, yes, she does help you in some ways. But the two of you are different—very different. She breaks the relationship. You go your own ways. Heartbroken, perhaps…But better off for it.

"You live high on a hill overlooking a garden. You have friends through work and the church you attend, you've got a good job, and you're an author—trade journals, I guess. You date another woman but only for a short while…Something's not right. Certain times of the year you still struggle. You end that friendship. Until ahhh, at last…they put you on some new medicine—much like the one that works for you now—only better. And that medicine works very well for you, Christopher. Well, you still have one or two setbacks but nothing like the ones you've had here recently. Oh, if we only had those medicines today.

"I don't want to say a lot about relationships, Christopher, but yes you do marry. Yes, quite close by with all of your family present. You have a good wife. She helps you in certain situations and you help her, too. The two of you are a good match... You come into money. Let's see—would that be a lot of money by today's standard? Yes, it would. You decide to move from your home high on the hill overlooking a garden. I don't know why you'd choose to move but you do. You don't move far, just a short distance... And the two of you—you and your wife—do some traveling. To some nice places I might add... You're active in the Church, much like your father. You rise quite high in that Church.

"I'm not going to say much of anything about children, Christopher. But before you and your wife have a child—think about what you've been through. Are you sure you want to bring a child into this world? I'm not going to say anything more. But keep in mind that the world has become a very scary place, here in the U.S. as well as abroad. Maybe you could stop some of the violence if I told you more. But no, who'd believe you?

"Now in your forties—you have no major setbacks...You manage projects each day at work. You're not very happy with your job. But you work hard, you do good work, and they pay you very well... You look young and healthy. But no, you have a stroke, no, not a stroke. The symptoms of a stroke but no, it's Bell's palsy. You heal. No neurological damage.

"And what? You move again. This time cross country...I'm not sure you should do this, Christopher. You don't know anyone where you're going. And yet you and your wife up and move... Well, let's see how this works out. At this new location you and your wife make friends, but you're shuffled around some at work, until at last—yes, they let you go. A re-organization, I guess... Let's think about this—you're oh about 45 years old, you've lost your job, the economy is bad—you're hundreds of miles from your family back east—yet you smile even as they give you notice...But it's not quite that simple. You can't move. They're building a house—a foundation—just a few feet from your home. Who'd buy it now?

"And yet wait—you're still there—working at that same place but in a different part of the company. You work harder than ever at your new job, but you never should have accepted this position. A year or two pass and they let you go again. You should've known something or done something different? Some issue or another with your medicines? In any case, they let you go. Now where do you turn?

"Let's see, spring turns to summer... Finally, you land a contract and then full-time work. You don't fall far but that full-time position doesn't last. You've cut back on your meds. At work, you make a mistake and try to cover it up. You own up to your mistake, but it's too late. Your manager leaves the company and they disband your unit. Your position is terminated...If nothing else, Christopher, remember this...you must stay on your meds—on all of your meds—exactly as prescribed...

"You need to find a job. The economy is at its worst since the Great Depression. Some men would take their lives in your situation, but no—not you. You keep fighting. You send your resume to recruiters and employers all around the country by computer. You even have one of those things—a computer—in your very own home. It all seems a bit strange—but times have changed. Let's go on...

"In the end, you put your home on the market and return to Massachusetts. Yes, you and your wife finally return home. Finding a job in the Boston area won't be easy—all of your professional contacts are back where you came from. But your family and friends are glad you're back east. You live with your mother in the house you grew up in. She takes you in. Despite all of your troubles—you're very fortunate, Christopher—you have a great mother...You can't stay in her home for a long time—just long enough to sell your old home and find a place of your own. Moreover, you need to find work. You have good work experience, but you've been without a job for some time. Employers aren't quite sure what to do with you—the job market for healthcare professionals is particularly tight in Massachusetts...

"At last, you find work with a small insurance company in the city. You move from your mother's home and buy a house of your own. A good neighborhood, a nice home—with a swimming pool in the back…But you still have issues with your medicines. I see—yes, your doctor wants to take you off the Lithium Carbonate. The Lithium is affecting your physical health—your kidneys… They lower your dosage and put you on another medicine, but the transition to the new meds fails. Your work performance declines. Your employer lets you go a few months later.

"You need to find work, Christopher. You have many bills and expenses each month. You submit your resume to some companies and you do some interviewing. Your doctors try once again to wean you off the Lithium Carbonate. And this time they succeed…The transition is—well—somewhat rough, but you seem much healthier without the Lithium. You need to stay on your new medicines, Christopher—you need to stay on all of them. Especially the one that works best for you…You lose some weight. And yes, you look great. I would think many employers would hire someone with your looks and skills. But no, you are still unemployed.

"Ah, yes, now I see. You're writing a story… And yes, you do write well. You write a story about your life. Not just any story—a good story at that. Much more balanced than your first story… And yes, you eventually do find some success with your writing. But you still need a job, Christopher—anything to pay the bills—and the job market remains tight. Months go by…Some claim the end of times is near, but the end of the world doesn't happen—not in your lifetime…Let's think about this—what could Christopher do? Some friends suggest that you enter politics, but don't do it, Christopher. You care too much. You'd be crushed. You can't be a policeman or a fireman…You could be a teacher like your mother, but no—you're capable of much more. Sales perhaps…Yes, the world could certainly use a few more honest salesmen.

"Let's turn forward a bit and see how this all works out in the end…You find new work in your field not far from the school you once attended…Your worst of times are over in terms of your mood swings and mental illness. You have issues occasionally with your medicines—but they are minor by comparison.

"Several years pass. Your kidney function has declined. You have to have surgery. The doctors remove a cyst from your kidney and at last, after a few years, they give you a new kidney. You have other complications as well, apnea and a brush with skin cancer. A modern-day Job, you just keep going.

"You retire. In retirement you live comfortably and do some travelling. You have a heart attack which slows you down—and another years later. You have a long life and a good wife—despite all the difficulties she stays with you to the end...

"That's all I have to say, Christopher. Overall, I'd say you have a good, long life—much better than most of my patients. You can rest comfortably as you leave this world. You've helped some people in your lifetime—people like you—those with your condition... There's not much else to say. You see, all you have is this one life, Christopher. Nothing more... So do the best you can with what you have. That's all you can do.

"Now I want you to slowly—ever so gradually—open your eyes. That's it. Good. You will remember most everything I've spoken here today. Maybe not word for word, but as your life unfolds, you'll remember much of what I've said. So, keep these two things in mind—listen to your doctors—they're here to help you...and stay on your medicines. Think of it this way—the people around you—me, your parents, wife, friends, co-workers, therapists, and your pastors—we're all here trying to help you. We all want you to succeed. Now, I want you to slowly open your eyes and think about what you've heard today. If your life is true to this foretelling then you will indeed have something to write about. But if you mention my name and this foretelling to your parents or anyone else, I will outright deny it. That is, if I'm still alive."

| # Without Looking Back

I return to college in the fall, study diligently most days and nights, and complete my Bachelor's degree at the University of Massachusetts in May, 1986. Family and a few friends from my freshman year at Brown attend the graduation ceremony. It is a proud moment. That summer I live at home with my parents in Topsfield. I work at a local program for adults with developmental disabilities. Assisting these persons is rewarding at times but the work is physically and emotionally draining.

I receive an assistantship and start graduate studies at the University of North Carolina at Chapel Hill that fall. The graduate coursework in healthcare administration is interesting and the studies challenge me. But I often do not feel confident—in control of my thoughts, my emotions, myself. Sometimes I act and pray like a man of God. Other times I am simply a child.

I stay devoutly on my medicines. Nonetheless I fall ill that spring while attending a meeting for public health interns in Rockville, Maryland. I'm hospitalized at a county psychiatric facility in Rockville for two weeks. My meds are adjusted and I quickly regain sanity. Two of my friends from Brown, Joe and Fred, visit me there. They drive me to the airport and get me on a plane back to Raleigh. I feel ashamed by the hospitalization. I've embarrassed my graduate school program and my fellow students. I relapse—having left the psychiatric facility in Maryland too soon. I'm hospitalized at North Carolina Memorial Hospital for three weeks—shortly after resuming coursework in Chapel Hill. I finish my studies for the semester that summer. Professors and my fellow students are polite and understanding of my health issues, but I am devastated. My friends pity me. I am handicapped by my illness. God, how can this be? Will I ever amount to anything?

Dad drives down to visit me in Chapel Hill. His face looks forlorn and weary. The once thick black hair on the top of his head is thin and graying. The space in his eyes grows deeper. Together we decide that I should take a leave of absence from school. I return home to Topsfield—a defeated man. Dear Lord, please be with me…I'm out of school—25 years old—still living at home with my parents. I feel like a failure. Why God? Why do these things have to happen to me? What did I do to deserve this?

The whole situation is more than a little frustrating. Each night at home my dad asks me if I've taken my medicines. This annoys me. I feel like a child. On the other hand, he's right. I need to take my daily dosage of Lithium Carbonate and Haldol every night before going to bed. I can't go for more than a few weeks without taking my medicines, or I may risk relapse. Dad has a smile for most everyone in public, but not always at home for his own family. Mom, Dad, and I play card games like Skip-Bo and cribbage a few nights each week. Dad and I compete when playing these games. He's a tough competitor. When he wants to win the game, he does. And when he wins repeatedly, I sometimes feel cheated.

Dad's health takes a turn for the worse that fall. Dad tells me he has adult-onset diabetes though he has never been seen by a doctor. I hear his words of lament. He frequently mentions how my mom and I must stick together and care for each other after he's gone. He often speaks of the world as against him, that you can't trust anyone—that no one really gives a damn.

That fall I accept a position managing data for an Alzheimer's research program in East Boston. Dad drops me off at the train station in Beverly, Massachusetts one snowy December morning.

As we approach the station, Dad and I quarrel over some change that's fallen to the floorboard. Dad tells me twice to pick up the nickel. I ask him to please just get me to the station. I'll be late for work if I don't catch the 7:20 train to Boston. I unlock the car door as we approach the station.

"Just remember this, Chris. You may think you're different, but you're not. You, me, we all have problems. I won't be around to help you forever and yes; some people will try to take advantage of you. But no one can make you do anything unless you let them. Whatever you do in this life, Chris, just remember—it's your nickel."

I run to make the train. I get to work on time. Dad has a heart attack while shovelling snow a few hours later. I never see him again alive. My brothers and I speak at the funeral service. Together we carry the coffin. I have lost my father—my greatest champion—a chapter from a story long foretold in my past. Dad is gone to a better place for sure—but gone. My mom is shaken by the loss of her husband but she assures me that she is fine on her own.

I receive a new graduate assistantship and return to the University of North Carolina at Chapel Hill the following November. I'm either in class, studying, or at work most weekdays and weeknights. On weekends, I play racquetball and video games, and party with my housemates and their friends. Life is good. I stay on my meds as prescribed and I'm happy—but not for long.

The pressures at school are great—sometimes overwhelming. I know I'm smart enough to do the work and earn my degree—but at times my concentration is fogged by the Haldol, hindering my ability to focus on studies. I remain devoutly on my meds, but midway through the spring semester I fall ill and have back-to-back hospitalizations at Duke Hospital and North Carolina Memorial Hospital. I'm embarrassed by these failures, but I'm determined to complete my graduate studies. I rebound, study both day and night, and earn my master's degree from the University of North Carolina in May, 1991.

After graduation, I move to Bowie, Maryland. My brother and sister-in-law take me in while I look for work and a place to live. Three months later I find full-time employment as a planning analyst at a healthcare organization in Washington, DC. I accept another position with a health insurance trade association the following year. I make friends through work and I participate each week in a young adult program at Christ Congregational Church in Silver Spring, Maryland. I make new friends through the church, but my relationship with God is needy. I call upon Him when I am weak and alone. And I am weak and alone much of the time. I often feel weary and distant—a common side-effect of my medicines. The lethargy, the shakiness, the incessant need to urinate each hour of the day and night—I despise the side effects…but I can't cope without the meds.

The following year I start dating a woman who works across the hall from my office. She is Sri Lankan. I had shied away from women almost entirely before meeting her. Plagued by illness, I can't see how any woman would be interested in me. The two of us go out to eat at local restaurants and occasionally we see movies together. We become best friends. Outside of family and my doctors, Dee is the first person I confide in about my bipolar condition. We talk a lot about my hospitalizations and the painful experiences that led to them. She listens.

In 1996, I fall ill while on a business trip in Dallas, Texas. It's the first time that I've been hospitalized in almost five years. My meds are adjusted—and my lithium level stabilizes. As I regain reason, I'm embarrassed by the setback. Moreover, I'm concerned about how the hospitalization may impact my career. While at the facility in Fort Worth, I get permission to call my manager at work. My manager assures me that my job at the trade association is secure. I feel energized with that reassurance, but I remain hospitalized for ten days.

My girlfriend Dee visits me the day I return home from Texas. She brings me dinner from a local restaurant, makes sure I have medicines and that I'm okay on my own. We are best friends, but the two of us are different—very different. She has many friends and is sociable, while I am quieter and more reserved. Within a few weeks, Dee finds a new boyfriend. We go our separate ways. I've lost my best friend—my most trusted friend. I am torn.

A year later—following several days of extreme nausea—I am hospitalized for three days while my medicines are adjusted. I feel exhausted—yet relieved that my hospital stay is brief. Within a few months I start dating another woman, Jennifer. The two of us eat at local restaurants and we frequently go to church together. As we become better friends, I feel I must tell Jennifer about my bipolar condition—but I'm afraid to do so. If I tell her, what are the odds that she'll reject me? My friendship with Jennifer lasts just three months. I break the relationship with Jennifer much like Dee broke relations with me the year before. Given my illnesses, their recurrence and my fears of rejection, I'm afraid of getting into a more serious relationship. I am a coward—once again weak and alone.

October, 1998. I'm anxious and reeling. Illness rages within me despite the fact that I remain staunchly on my meds. It takes all of my strength to contain the mania. I'm physically sick and emotionally tattered. I haven't slept in days. My thoughts spiral and escalate—connecting in bizarre and delusional ways. The world is against me. I can't trust anyone. Everyone at work is out to get me. Dear God, where are you? I fear for my life…

As a last resort, I walk to the office of my primary care physician three blocks from my home. I open the door. The nurse receptionist greets me with a warm hello as if we were old friends. I approach the front desk without making eye contact. I tell the nurse my name and remove from my wallet my insurance card and the business card of my psychiatrist. The nurse asks me for the reason of my visit. I hand her the business card and I tell her I'm sick. She reads the card, stares into my eyes for several moments and directs me into an examining room at the back of the office.

I sit alone silent in the examining room for what seems like an eternity. Ideas cast rampantly about my brain. My mind cannot keep pace. I'm all-powerful one moment—I'm weak, dazed and alone the next. Sick, sicker, weak, weaker, failing, failing, failed—at last, Dr. Gilbert arrives. He hands me two pills in a paper thimble and water in a paper cup. I pop the pills in my mouth and drink from the cup. Emotions that spring back and forth from extreme power to total fear gradually dispel—transient thoughts that revolve quickly and randomly slowly dissipate. I leave the doctor's office three hours later—exhausted. I walk home, close the window blinds in my bedroom, and lay down in bed. I sleep for the first time in three days.

The next afternoon I call Dr. Furst, my therapist, to tell him of my illness. Dr. Furst tells me he won't be seeing me much longer—too much red tape with my insurance company over the Zyprexa prescription. In the weeks that follow—the new regimen of Zyprexa and Lithium Carbonate relieves much of the lethargy I experienced while on Haldol. At work, I'm focused and better able to concentrate on projects. Among friends, I'm relaxed and more alert. Another episode from a story long foretold comes to a close.

Chapter 6 | Without Remorse

As the years pass, I rarely think about Dr. Stabler—or the story he foretold about me. But I realize my life is unfolding much as he said it would. I unwittingly trace the shadows of his foretelling time and again as I muddle from young adulthood through middle age. Parallels between his plan and certain events in my life are anything but random—they are frequent, sometimes disconcerting, and in an odd way reassuring. So, am I leading life? Is it God's plan for me, or am I simply following the script prescribed by my therapist? I don't understand it. I can't comprehend it. How could anyone foresee the future? It makes no sense.

I become a member at Fourth Presbyterian Church in Bethesda, Maryland in 1999. I serve there as an usher and a few years later as a deacon. Each Sunday morning, I participate in a Bible study. I sit among persons who are much older and wiser than me. One Sunday morning the woman next to me tells me something I'm sure I've heard a thousand times or more.

"Chris, if you confess your sins to Jesus Christ your sins and transgressions will be forgiven. You may not be able to forgive yourself or deal with your own guilt. But the Lord will see you as free of blame."

Jane is right. Over time I pray, I confess my sins and transgressions and I find strength in God's sight. I turn my failures over to God. I begin to forgive myself for my chemical imbalance and the many episodes that have come with it. After all, who am

I—a believer—not to accept God's forgiveness as my own? The seeds of illness, anguish and guilt lose their sting. My weaknesses become my strengths. I find confidence and joy in the Lord. I realign my trust in Him alone.

I start new employment with a health insurance plan in Rockville, Maryland in 2001. I manage health care projects with colleagues and medical professionals from outside the company. My manager resigns her post and I assume many of her work assignments on an interim basis. I take on significantly more responsibility, remain dutiful to the cause and I am paid commensurately.

I meet a young woman, Melissa Bell, at a Church picnic that summer. We start dating soon thereafter. I find Melissa fun to be around, intelligent and very attractive. Melissa is tall, of medium build with long blonde hair that reaches just past her shoulders. I visit Melissa each weekend at her home in McLean, Virginia. She laughs at my subtle humor—we cry together on 9/11. I don't tell Melissa of my bipolar condition. I fear that if she knew, she might end our friendship.

August 29, 2002. Today is Melissa's thirtieth birthday. We've been dating for a little more than a year. Now I must tell her. I want to marry her.

"Melissa, I love you... and I want to spend the rest of my life with you. But there's something you don't know about me. I'm bipolar..."

Melissa looks curiously into my eyes for several moments. I brace myself—anticipating rejection. Without speaking she dismisses my fears with a kiss and loving embrace.

We plan a small wedding—inviting only immediate family and a few of our closest friends. Melissa and I marry the day after Christmas in my hometown of Topsfield, Massachusetts. We spend our wedding night at a bed and breakfast in Gloucester, Massachusetts and honeymoon several months later at Disneyworld in Orlando, Florida. We come into money through employment stock options and travel to London, Paris and the Caribbean despite the realities of global violence and terrorism. We move from our one-bedroom condominium which sits high on a hill overlooking a garden to a small single-family home in Silver Spring, Maryland. I feel more loved and at peace than I have in twenty years—but love is not a panacea for bipolar disorder as Melissa and I would soon learn.

Late September 2003. Two nights without sleep—I'm wired beyond exhaustion. I sit up in bed. Melissa lies quietly by my side. Tangled ideas loop endlessly about my mind. One moment I'm angry at persons whose hurtful words echo in my memory. The next minute I'm full of fear—certain that I'll lose my job because of something I've said, or something I didn't say at work. I look at the alarm clock on the nightstand. It's 10:30 pm. I don't know what to do. I can't call my psychiatrist—she might try to admit me. And if that were to happen, I'd surely lose my job. I hear a soft voice beside me.

"Chris, I'm worried about you. You're not sleeping again tonight. Let's go to the hospital now—before it gets too late. You need help..."

"No, Melissa. I don't need to go to the hospital. I can get through this myself."

"Chris—please...this has been going on for two nights now. Please, let's just get in the car and drive down the street to Holy Cross."

"No, Melissa, I won't go. I don't need to —"

Melissa doesn't back down. Our conversation circles for the better part of an hour. At last, I agree to visit the emergency room at Holy Cross Hospital—less than a mile from our home in Silver Spring, Maryland. My mind is not right as we enter the door to the emergency room. I feel weak and fatigued. There are already thirty or more patients waiting ahead of us in line. There are babies crying. There are children sleeping on the laps of their parents. There are older men and women—their faces tired, forlorn and pale. Melissa and I wait patiently. She fills out some paperwork while I do my best to gather my thoughts. I know I'm not well. I have to be at my best, or risk being admitted to the county psychiatric facility in Rockville, Maryland.

"My name is Christopher Holdstrom. This is my wife, Melissa. I was first diagnosed as bipolar in 1981…and I'm not well tonight. My thoughts race and I know I need sleep. I take Lithium Carbonate and 5 mg of Zyprexa each night before going to bed. If I increase my dosage of Zyprexa tonight, I'll get the sleep I need… I don't need to be hospitalized…"

The doctor at the emergency room is a big man with black horn-rimmed glasses. He glances over the paperwork that Melissa's filled out while listening attentively to my words.

"Mr. Holdstrom, have you taken your Zyprexa tonight?"

"No, sir. Not yet."

"It's almost midnight, Mr. Holdstrom. I want you to take your meds now…I want you to take 10 mg of Zyprexa—twice your usual dosage. Do you understand me, Mr. Holdstrom?"

"Yes, sir. I do."

"Do you have your meds with you here tonight, Mr. Holdstrom?"

"Yes, sir. I do."

"Okay. Hand them to me."

I grab a handful of prescription bottles from my coat pocket.

"Wait here a minute, Mr. Holdstrom. Let me get you a cup of water."

The doctor returns with two pills in a paper thimble and water in a paper cup. I pop the pills in my mouth, and drink from the cup. He nods approvingly.

"Mrs. Holdstrom, I want you to take Mr. Holdstrom to see his doctor first thing tomorrow morning. Can you do that for me?"

"Yes. I'll take Chris to see his doctor first thing tomorrow—"

Melissa drives me home that night. The double dose of Zyprexa knocks me out soon after we lay down in bed. I sleep through the night. I meet with my medication manager the next day. Within a week my sleep pattern steadily corrects to eight hours each night under the new regimen of Zyprexa. I feel lethargic much of the time, but the mania subsides. Were it not for Melissa's diligence in getting me to the emergency room that night—the outcome may have been very different.

Months pass. I awake in bed one morning in April. It's Sunday—time to get ready for Church. I roll from bed to my feet, stretch, and lumber slowly down the carpeted stairs toward the bathroom on the first floor. I look at my reflection in the mirror and try to muster a smile. The expression on the right side of my face is flat—I'm unable to smile—and I can't close my right eyelid. A rush of fear floods my mind and body—my immediate thought is stroke. Within a minute—Melissa and I dress and race for the car. I'm examined by a team of doctors and nurses at INOVA Hospital for several hours that day. In the end, the doctors rule out stroke and diagnose me with Bell's palsy. I'd heard of the disorder in the past, many years before. I'm relieved to learn that the condition will most likely dissipate on its own and in fact; the disconcerting paralysis heals over the course of three weeks. For me, it's another chapter from a story long foretold in my past.

Melissa becomes pregnant in 2006. We are thrilled as are family and friends. A career opportunity arises for me and we decide to relocate to Minnesota. It's a great and awesome adventure. All of our family is back east. We have no friends in the Twin Cities area. But we make friends soon after relocating. Melissa and I become members at Faith Presbyterian Church in Minnetonka, Minnesota in November. I later become a Stephen Minister in that Church.

God blesses us with a healthy baby daughter on February 2, 2007. Suzanna is small and precious. Her hands and feet are tiny, her head is bald, and her cry is resilient and strong. She cries by day. She coos at night. She brings us joy and hope for the future.

I work at a national health insurance company in Edina, Minnesota. My position as project manager is more demanding than any job that I've held previously. Moreover, the side effects from my meds are oppressive. I often feel fogged and frustrated by my inability to concentrate at work. My hands tremble—most excruciatingly when I lead discussions at weekly business meetings—I need to pee every hour of the day and night—and my lower back and kidneys ache periodically. The job is challenging. I need to do my best work, but I can't do my best given the side effects. The company I work for experiences funding constraints and my division is downsized in August. I'm left without employment. Dear Lord, how could this happen? How could they let me go? If it weren't for the meds—the side effects—I'd still have a job. But now I have nothing…How long can my family get by with me being out of work?

Two weeks later I'm hired back within that same company but in a different department. I'm tasked with leading a large project team through a critical, long-term initiative. I was let go once. I can't lose my job again. My family is counting on me and my income... While I'm cautious with my meds and wary of tampering with them—the pressures at work continue to mount. I need to concentrate. I need to be more focused and alert. I can do the work. I'd do just fine if it weren't for the meds…I take calculated risks, cutting back slightly on the Lithium Carbonate when I feel overmedicated and distant. But I tell no one. I don't need to burden anyone with this. This is a minor correction. My therapist, Dr. Beauchamp? Would he understand? No, how could he? I can get through this myself. This is my business. I'll be fine…

I'm far too stubborn—and much too proud. Cutting back on my meds creates new, more daunting challenges. I feel more alert, more capable at work and my hand tremors diminish somewhat—but mild bouts of mania surface. Melissa watches over me. She knows when I don't sleep at night. Together, we visit my doctor when my thoughts accelerate.

Work requires long hours of unpaid overtime. A year passes and I receive an award from the company for my service. But periodic stints of mania persist. My manager—unaware of my bipolar condition—cautions me about a sudden downward break in my work performance in January. He suggests that I participate in an employee assistance program. I refuse his advice and within three weeks I'm asked to resign. I'm more than a little angered by the job loss, and it takes four months for me to find new employment as a temporary contractor.

I land a full-time position at another healthcare firm that October, but that full-time position doesn't last. I misplace my laptop at work and instead of admitting my error—I try to cover my mistake. Within a few days, I admit my foolishness. My hiring manager leaves the company, and the unit I work in is disbanded. My position as project manager is terminated in the reorganization that follows. I can only reflect on my demise. Dear God, please be with me…I've lost my job twice in less than a year. I've placed my family at financial risk. If I'd just stayed on my meds as directed the entire episode might have been averted—and I'd still be employed. I feel like an idiot. I've been warned countless times about tampering with my meds. But the side effects—my inability to concentrate—my physical health…What else could I do? I become depressed and disgusted with myself. I pried with my meds—I'm responsible for my recent job losses.

Melissa and I decide to put our home on the market and relocate. In April, we move cross-country to my hometown of Topsfield, Massachusetts to be closer to family. My Mom takes us in while Melissa and I look to find work and re-settle. Our three-year old daughter, Suzanna, attends a local preschool. She often plays outdoors with friends—her long strawberry blonde hair shines in the summer sun.

Many say the country is in its worst economic times since the Great Depression. Massachusetts is in the midst of recession and health care reform—the job market for healthcare professionals is particularly tight. Melissa finds work at Harvard Law School; we sell our home in Minnesota and I find work as a business analyst in Boston, Massachusetts in November. We purchase a property in Braintree, Massachusetts—a modest home with a swimming pool—and a big mortgage. Our transition from Minnesota to Braintree has taken almost a year, but we're glad to be settled in our new home close to family.

In September, 2011—my medication manager advises that I see a specialist to discuss some recent lab results. I drive myself to Addison Gilbert Hospital one cloudy Saturday morning. This time I will not be hospitalized. Walker II is gone. I visit Radiology Services to have my kidneys checked by sonogram. Two weeks later, I review the test results with a nephrologist. I am diagnosed with stage 3 chronic kidney disease. The nephrologist explains to me that the long-term effects of the Lithium Carbonate could very well lead to renal failure even if I were to stop taking the Lithium today.

It's all too ironic. That same medicine that kept me free from a life of institutionalization and mental demise—now threatens to rob me of my physical health and well-being. Going forward, meds must not only contain my bipolar affective disorder—they must also balance the risk of potential renal failure. For me, it's another episode from a story long foretold.

Together, my medication manager and nephrologist agree that I must be weaned off the Lithium Carbonate immediately. My daily dosage of Lithium is cut, and I start a new regimen of Zyprexa with Depakote as a substitute for the Lithium Carbonate. My concentration wanes. My work performance declines. My annual employee evaluation reflects the demise. In June 2012, my position at work is terminated. In an exit interview, I'm told that funding constraints led to my layoff. I feel defeated and depressed—once again I've failed my wife and daughter.

Out of work, I spend most days running errands, doing chores around the house and looking for new employment. I'm temporarily placed on my former regimen of Lithium Carbonate and Zyprexa. Each morning as I sit at home alone, I set aside two hours to do nothing but write. I write a story about my past. That story consumes much of my being—I'm haunted by my past mistakes and transgressions. I meet with a new medication manager, Ruth, that July. She too advises that I transition off the Lithium Carbonate to prevent further kidney damage. She puts me on a new regimen of meds including Zyprexa, Abilify and Lamictal. In the days that follow, I do not sleep many hours each night. My appetite fades. I become more irritable and aloof.

Melissa notices the abrupt change in my mood. We quarrel one Sunday morning as she drives me and Suzanna home from church. "Chris, I know you're not sleeping at night. I think you should see your doctor right away." I reply indignantly, "I will not go to the hospital." I reach quickly to my left, grab the steering wheel, and turn off the ignition. The Corolla coasts to a stop by the side of a roundabout. Melissa hastily turns the key to the ignition and shifts gears. The car surges forward. Again, I plead, "No, I will not go to the hospital." Melissa points in the direction of the Harvard Vanguard medical building some distance away, "I'm taking you there, Chris." Again, I reach to my left, grab the steering wheel, and turn off the ignition. Melissa cries out angrily, "We're not going anywhere, Chris…I'm taking you home!"

Sleeplessness persists. I don't sleep for more than an hour that night. Melissa and I meet with my medication manager at Harvard Vanguard the next day. Ruth increases my daily dosage of Zyprexa. She recommends that I participate in a day program at Arbour Counselling Services in Boston, Massachusetts. On Friday morning, Melissa drives me to Arbour. Together, we fill out the paper work for beginning the day program. I don't remember much of my first days at Arbour Counselling Services. My brain is fogged from lack of sleep and the heightened medication regimen. I participate in meetings at the day program each of the next nine weekdays. Clients at the day program come and go. We talk about self-esteem and relationships. I realize we all have problems. I feel a little more alert with each passing day but I still have periods of dizziness and listlessness from the meds.

I'm at home with Melissa and Suzanna in the evenings and on weekends—healing that no hospital can afford. Though I'm not hospitalized—I am not well. I suffer mild bouts of paranoia due to the sudden withdrawal from the Lithium. The periodic ache that once wrenched my kidneys is gone, but I lie awake in bed most nights crying—full of anger and fear. Anger towards those whose once hurtful words rage in my memory. Fear that my once secure career may now have crumbled beyond repair.

Prayer is my only refuge. Dear Lord, please be with me…I'm in poor health—without work —and our family savings dwindle. I've traced Dr. Stabler's foretelling—the very plan he shared with me more than two decades ago. How could this happen? How can this be?

Melissa and Suzanna hear my words and cries of frustration each night. They lay quietly in bed in the next room hoping it all will pass.

My mind gradually adjusts to the new regimen of medicines. In November, I accept seasonal employment with a national jewellery store in Braintree as a sales associate. I study the company manual and pass all the tests—but I still feel out of place much of the time while working the sales floor. That position closes just after the holidays.

I network with recruiters and former colleagues. At last, I land a contract with a health information consulting firm in April. I manage the implementation of a financial management system for a healthcare reform project in Rhode Island. Our office is in Rumford, Rhode Island just a few miles my old stomping ground at Brown University. The work is challenging and interesting. I come to realize that, with this employment, I've unwittingly traced the foretelling that Dr. Stabler shared with me more than twenty-five years ago.

I had a psychotic episode at age nineteen. Without sleep and sustenance—I lost all reason. I overcame that hell thanks to God and the care that I received through Dr. Stabler and his staff at Addison Gilbert Hospital. Diagnosed with bipolar affective disorder, I was placed on a regimen of Lithium Carbonate and Haldol. Were it not for those medicines I might well have been institutionalized for life. With those meds, I regained both reason and my freedom within a span of forty days.

The Lithium Carbonate and Haldol, however, were not a cure-all. I struggled with their side effects, and in turn I suffered three hospitalizations in four years. Dr. Stabler was my therapist and medication manager through much of that time. I sat quietly in his office one sunny, fall day—mesmerized—an unknowing spectator tracing shadows in time.

Dr. Stabler told me a story that afternoon that set me on a journey. That journey would span more than two decades. I can't recall his plan for me word-for-word—over the years details of the foretelling fade. But I still hear the cadence of his Boston accent, and on rare occasion the very words he spoke spill into consciousness. Dr. Stabler's foretelling was far removed from the future I envisioned for myself. Yet over the years I unintentionally traced his story much as he said I would. I no longer obsess over his prophecy—or how I may have unwittingly followed his plan. It never has and I suspect that it never will make any sense to me.

One thing is clear. God is my one and only true anchor through times of adversity. No matter how bad the circumstance—at times when I might rightfully have given up—I've found a glimmer of strength and reassurance in Him through prayer. I learned to love God as a child. He created me for a reason—somehow, He would use me. I would never know God's plan for me in this lifetime, but

I'd follow His plan so long as I prayed to Him for direction. I never thought much about the Lord's plan for me but I had confidence that God would watch over me and protect me.

Perhaps someday, God's plan for me will make total sense. But for now, I wait and ponder. Leading life or being led—I am not who I was. Mine is yet a plan undone.

> *Trust in the Lord with all your heart,*
> *and do not lean on your own understanding.*
> *In all ways acknowledge him,*
> *and he will make straight your paths.*

> -Proverbs 3:5-6 (NIV)

Epilogue

Thanksgiving Day, 2022. I count my blessings. I'm indebted to those who have helped guide me through a maze that simply became more complex through the years—most notably my wife Melissa, my daughter Suzanna, my mom and dad, and my brothers and their families. I'm thankful also for the reassuring wisdom, advice and encouragement I've received through pastors and from friends, therapists, counselors, and medication managers. I'm also grateful for the Abilify and Lamictal that help contain my chemical imbalance. These meds are not a cure, but they are a blessing. I expect that I'll remain on these—or similar medicines—for the rest of my life.

While my mood swings and mental illness are now effectively contained by the meds, my doctors face the formidable challenge of finding a chemical supplement to balance my bipolar and renal conditions. In 2021, my diagnosis was relegated to stage 4 chronic kidney disease after a cyst was removed from my left kidney. I have been on peritoneal dialysis ever since. To stay alive, I must undergo dialysis each night as I sleep at home in bed. In addition, I have been diagnosed with melanoma and sleep apnea.

I am frequently plagued by guilt and regret as I lie awake in bed at night. I sometimes wallow in self-pity for hours—thinking about what might have been had only this or that not happened in my past. Such rubbish tends to magnify over time. I find that prayer is most effective in dispelling such nonsense.

All and all I feel fortunate and blessed to be alive and to share my story. Writing this book has been a cathartic and liberating process. I hope the story may benefit others and their loved ones as well.

God be with me—I will start anew. This is my time. I feel free...